Hymns as Poetry

St Ippolyt's. *From an etching by F L Griggs*

Hymns as Poetry

edited by Samuel Carr

Preface by John Betjeman

BT BATSFORD LTD, LONDON

FIRST PUBLISHED 1980
SELECTION © SAMUEL CARR 1980
ISBN 0 7134 3447 3
FILMSET IN MONOPHOTO PLANTIN LIGHT BY
SERVIS FILMSETTING LTD, MANCHESTER
PRINTED BY
FAKENHAM PRESS LTD
FAKENHAM, NORFOLK
FOR THE PUBLISHERS B T BATSFORD LTD,
4 FITZHARDINGE STREET, LONDON W1H OAH

The front endpaper, Adam and Eve driven out of Paradise, is from a mezzotint engraving by John Martin (1789–1854). *William Weston Gallery, London.* The back endpaper, The Great Day of his Wrath, is reproduced from a painting by John Martin. *The Tate Gallery, London*

Contents

RIGHT A Village Choir. *Thomas Webster*

Preface

It can't be poetry, it's only a hymn.

It is very difficult to get away from the *tunes* of hymns once they are in the head, and they are in most of our heads.

This selection has been made by my friend Sam Carr with the idea of reading hymns as poems and forgetting the tunes.

Our greatest religious poet is Blake. He alone seems to have expressed the Deity in rhythm and metre without being commonplace. In the seventeenth century there were some great poets who wrote religious lyrics: George Herbert, Richard Baxter, Richard Crashaw, Milton, John Byrom. The subject was not too big for them. Isaac Watts is to me the outstanding seventeenth-century hymn writer:

> *When I survey the wondrous Cross*
> *Where the young Prince of glory died.*

The older seventeenth-century lines are, as in this case, often more striking than Victorian revisions of them. That fierce Calvinist, Augustus Montague Toplady (an old Westminster) wrote a final verse to 'Rock of Ages' which was too much for Victorian imaginings:

> *While I draw this fleeting breath,*
> *When my eyestrings break in death.*

LEFT St Andrew's, Plymouth. *From an engraving after Thomas Allom by F Dixc*

This is where English painting, except for Blake, Samuel Palmer and some of the medieval illuminators, falls short of the standards set by seventeenth-century hymn writers. In the painting of sacred subjects there was an almost total gap of about two and a half centuries from the Reformation until Blake was to treat the theme with conviction again. The Pre-Raphaelites as painters seem to me smaller beer and more literary than such poetic giants as Milton.*

There were plenty of people who were good poets only as hymn writers, notably J M Neale. Another good poet is Mrs C F Alexander (whose country of Northern Ireland shines through 'All things bright and beautiful'). With some exceptions, such as Cecil Spring-Rice and Kipling's 'Recessional', there has been a decline in the present century in religious poetry, as in religious painting, but overall there is much indeed worth reading and looking at.

JOHN BETJEMAN

*Although many of us will agree with Dr Johnson's observation: '*Paradise Lost* is one of the books which the reader admires and lays down, and forgets to take up again. None ever wished it longer than it is. Its perusal is a duty rather than a pleasure.'

Editor's Note

The Editor's warm thanks are due to Sir John Betjeman, who suggested this book and who proposed many of the hymn writers who are represented in it. The Editor is also much indebted to the Rev J B Gaskell for his help in the choice of hymns.

As the Preface points out, many early hymns are familiar, not in their original form, but in a nineteenth-century recension. This presents a difficulty: should the authentic version be preferred to the one which most people will recognise? Since the collection is of hymns *as poetry* it seemed better in almost every case to print them as they were written, even though to do so may present the reader with some surprises and some disappointments. The punctuation and the use of capitals and italics have also reverted to that of the original authors. An exception has, however, been made in the case of length; occasionally, verses have been omitted so as to preserve the traditional extent.

The pictures are not intended as illustrations but rather as complements to the hymns. With the exception of the Wilton Diptych, which is believed to be French, they have been taken from works by British artists since however foreign in origin some of the hymns may have been, they are now unequivocally English. Even the psalms, of which one or two are here included, now seem English on account of the familiarity of the versions made of them by Miles Coverdale, and Tate and Brady.

The Editor and Publishers would like to thank the National Trust of Great Britain and Eyre Methuen Ltd for permission to reproduce Rudyard Kipling's hymn 'Recessional'.

SC

The Illustrations

Virgin and Child. *William Blake*

The holly and the ivy

The holly and the ivy,
    When they are both full grown,
Of all the trees that are in the wood,
    The holly bears the crown:

> *The rising of the sun*
> *And the running of the deer,*
> *The playing of the merry organ,*
> *Sweet singing in the choir.*

The holly bears a blossom,
    As white as the lily flower,
And Mary bore sweet Jesus Christ
    To be our sweet Saviour:

The holly bears a berry,
    As red as any blood,
And Mary bore sweet Jesus Christ
    To do poor sinners good:

The holly bears a prickle,
    As sharp as any thorn,
And Mary bore sweet Jesus Christ
    On Christmas Day in the morn:

The holly bears a bark,
    As bitter as any gall,
And Mary bore sweet Jesus Christ
    For to redeem us all:

The holly and the ivy,
    When they are both full grown,
Of all the trees that are in the wood,
    The holly bears the crown:

ANONYMOUS

Jerusalem the golden

Jerusalem the golden,
   With milk and honey blest,
Beneath thy contemplation
   Sink heart and voice opprest.
I know not, O I know not,
   What social joys are there,
What radiancy of glory,
   What light beyond compare.

They stand, those halls of Sion,
   Conjubilant with song,
And bright with many an Angel,
   And all the Martyr throng:
The Prince is ever in them,
   The daylight is serene,
The pastures of the blessèd
   Are decked in glorious sheen.

There is the throne of David,
   And there, from care released,
The song of them that triumph,
   The shout of them that feast;
And they who, with their Leader,
   Have conquered in the fight,
For ever and for ever
   Are clad in robes of white.

O sweet and blessèd country,
   Shall I ever see thy face?
O sweet and blessèd country,
   Shall I ever win thy grace?
Exult, O dust and ashes!
   The Lord shall be thy part:
His only, his for ever,
   Thou shalt be, and thou art!

BERNARD OF CLUNY (twelfth century)
Translated by J M Neale (1818–1866)

Jerusalem. *From an engraving after J M W Turner by W Finden*

Ein' feste Burg

A safe stronghold our God is still,
 A trusty shield and weapon;
He'll help us clear from all the ill
 That hath us now o'ertaken.
  The ancient prince of hell
  Hath risen with purpose fell;
  Strong mail of craft and power
  He weareth in this hour;
On earth is not his fellow.

With force of arms we nothing can,
　　Full soon were we down-ridden;
But for us fights the proper Man,
　　Whom God himself hath bidden.
　　　　Ask ye, Who is this same?
　　　　Christ Jesus is his name,
　　　　The Lord Sabaoth's Son;
　　　　He, and no other one,
　　Shall conquer in the battle.

And were this world all devils o'er
　　And watching to devour us,
We lay it not to heart so sore;
　　Not they can overpower us.
　　　　And let the prince of ill
　　　　Look grim as e'er he will,
　　　　He harms us not a whit;
　　　　For why? – his doom is writ;
　　A word shall quickly slay him.

God's word, for all their craft and force,
　　One moment will not linger,
But, spite of hell, shall have its course;
　　'Tis written by his finger.
　　　　And though they take our life,
　　　　Goods, honour, children, wife,
　　　　Yet is their profit small;
　　　　These things shall vanish all,
　　The city of God remaineth.

MARTIN LUTHER (1483–1546)
　　translated by Thomas Carlyle (1795–1881)

The Last Supper. *Stanley Spencer*

PSALM 23: *The Lord is my shepherd*

The Lord is my shepherd; I shall not want.
He maketh me to lie down in green pastures:
He leadeth me beside the still waters.
He restoreth my soul:
He leadeth me in the paths of righteousness for his name's
    sake.
Yea, though I walk through the valley of the shadow of death,
I will fear no evil: for thou art with me;
Thy rod and thy staff they comfort me.
Thou preparest a table before me in the presence of mine
    enemies:
Thou anointest my head with oil; my cup runneth over.
Surely goodness and mercy shall follow me all the days of my
    life:
And I will dwell in the house of the Lord for ever.

Translated by Miles Coverdale (1488–1568)

The Good Shepherd. *George Richmond*

PSALM 121: *I will lift up mine eyes unto the hills*

I will lift up mine eyes unto the hills,
From whence cometh my help.
My help cometh from the Lord,
Which made heaven and earth.
He will not suffer thy foot to be moved:
He that keepeth thee will not slumber.
Behold, he that keepeth Israel
Shall neither slumber nor sleep.
The Lord is thy keeper:
The Lord is thy shade upon thy right hand.
The sun shall not smite thee by day,
Nor the moon by night.
The Lord shall preserve thee from all evil:
He shall preserve thy soul.
The Lord shall preserve thy going out and thy coming in
From this time forth, and even for evermore.

Translated by Miles Coverdale (1488–1568)

Ruth returning from the gleaning. *Samuel Palmer*

Most glorious Lord of life

Most glorious Lord of life, that on this day
Didst make thy triumph over death and sin,
And having harrowed hell, didst bring away
Captivity thence captive, us to win.

Most joyous day, dear Lord, with joy begin,
And grant that we for whom thou diddest die,
Being with thy dear Blood clean washed from sin,
May live for ever in felicity.

And that thy love we weighing worthily,
May likewise love thee for the same again,
And for thy sake, that all like dear didst buy,
With love may one another entertain.

So let us love, dear Love, like as we ought;
Love is the lesson which the Lord us taught.

EDMUND SPENSER (1553–1599)

Wilt thou forgive that sin

Wilt thou forgive that sin, by man begun,
   Which was my sin though it were done before?
Wilt thou forgive that sin, through which I run,
   And do run still, though still I do deplore?
When thou hast done, thou hast not done,
               For I have more.

Wilt thou forgive that sin which I have won
   Others to sin, and made my sin their door?
Wilt thou forgive that sin which I did shun
   A year or two, but wallowed in a score?
When thou hast done, thou hast not done,
               For I have more.

I have a sin of fear, that when I've spun
   My last thread, I shall perish on the shore,
But swear by thyself, that at my death thy Son
   Shall shine, as he shines now and heretofore:
And, having done that, thou hast done:
               I fear no more.

JOHN DONNE (1578–1631)

FROM: *His Letanie, to the Holy Spirit*

In the houre of my distress,
When temptations me oppresse,
And when I my sins confesse,
      Sweet Spirit comfort me!

When I lie within my bed,
Sick in heart, and sick in head,
And with doubts discomforted,
      Sweet Spirit comfort me!

When the house doth sigh and weep,
And the world is drown'd in sleep,
Yet mine eyes the watch do keep;
      Sweet Spirit comfort me!

When (God knowes) I'm tost about,
Either with despair, or doubt;
Yet before the glasse be out,
      Sweet Spirit comfort me!

When the Judgement is reveal'd,
And that open'd which was seal'd
When to thee I have appeal'd;
      Sweet Spirit comfort me!

ROBERT HERRICK (1591–1674)

Doom Painting at St Thomas's, Salisbury

Angeli Laudantes. *Edward Burne-Jones*

What sweeter music can we bring

What sweeter music can we bring
Than a carol, for to sing
The birth of this our heavenly King?
Awake the voice! Awake the string:

> *We see him once, and know him ours,*
> *Who with his sunshine and his showers*
> *Turns all the patient ground to flowers.*

Dark and dull night, fly hence away,
And give the honour to this day,
That sees December turned to May,
If we may ask the reason, say:

The darling of the world is come,
And fit it is we find a room
To welcome him. The nobler part
Of all the house here is the heart:

Which we will give him, and bequeath
This holly and this ivy wreath,
To do him honour who's our King,
And Lord of all this revelling.

ROBERT HERRICK (1591–1674)

I sing the birth was born to-night!

I sing the birth was born to-night,
The author both of life and light;
   The angels so did sound it,
And, like the ravished shepherds said,
Who saw the light, and were afraid,
   Yet searched, and true they found it.

The Son of God, the eternal King,
That did us all salvation bring,
   And freed our soul from danger,
He whom the whole world could not take,
The Word, which heaven and earth did make
   Was now laid in a manger.

The Father's wisdom willed it so,
The Son's obedience knew no No;
   Both wills were in one stature,
And, as that wisdom had decreed,
The Word was now made flesh indeed,
   And took on him our nature.

What comfort by him we do win,
Who made himself the price of sin,
   To make us heirs of glory!
To see this babe, all innocence,
A martyr born in our defence,
   Can man forget the story?

BEN JONSON (1573?–1637)

The Adoration. *Designed by Sir Edmund Burne-Jones*

Antiphon

Let all the world in ev'ry corner sing
   My God and King.
 The heav'ns are not too high,
 His praise may thither flye;
 The earth is not too low,
 His praises there may grow.
Let all the world in ev'ry corner sing
   My God and King.

 The church with psalms must shout,
 No door can keep them out:
 But above all, the heart
 Must bear the longest part.
Let all the world in ev'ry corner sing
   My God and King.

GEORGE HERBERT (1593–1632)

Angels. *From the 'Wilton Diptych'*

Come, Holy Ghost, our souls inspire

Come, Holy Ghost, our souls inspire,
And lighten with celestial fire;
Thou the anointing Spirit art,
Who dost thy sevenfold gifts impart:

Thy blessed unction from above
Is comfort, life, and fire of love;
Enable with perpetual light
The dullness of our blinded sight:

Anoint and cheer our soiled face
With the abundance of thy grace:
Keep far our foes, give peace at home;
Where thou art guide no ill can come.

Teach us to know the Father, Son,
And thee, of Both, to be but One;
That through the ages all along
This may be our endless song,
    Praise to thy eternal merit,
    Father, Son, and Holy Spirit.

BISHOP JOHN COSIN (1594–1672)
    (*After* Veni, Creator Spiritus)

The Dawn of Christianity. *J M W Turner*

The Lord will come and not be slow

The Lord will come and not be slow,
  His footsteps cannot err;
Before him righteousness shall go,
  His royal harbinger.

Truth from the earth, like to a flower,
  Shall bud and blossom then;
And justice, from her heavenly bower,
  Look down on mortal men.

Rise, God, judge thou the earth in might,
  This wicked earth redress;
For thou art he who shalt by right
  The nations all possess.

The nations all whom thou hast made
  Shall come, and all shall frame
To bow them low before thee, Lord,
  And glorify thy name.

For great thou art, and wonders great
  By thy strong hand are done:
Thou in thy everlasting seat
  Remainest God alone.

JOHN MILTON (1608–1674)
  (after Psalms 85–6)

Let us with a gladsom mind

Let us with a gladsom mind
Praise the Lord, for he is kind
   For his mercies ay endure,
   Ever faithful, ever sure.

Let us blaze his Name abroad,
For of gods he is the God:

He with all-commanding might
Filled the new-made world with light:

He the golden-tressèd sun
Caused all day his course to run:

The hornèd moon to shine by night,
'Mid her spangled sisters bright:

He his chosen race did bless
In the wasteful wilderness:

He hath, with a piteous eye,
Looked upon our misery:

All things living he doth feed,
His full hand supplies their need:

Let us, with a gladsom mind,
Praise the Lord, for he is kind:

JOHN MILTON (1608–1674)
  (after Psalm 136)

FROM: *A Hymn of the Nativity*

Gloomy Night embrac't the place
    Where the noble Infant lay:
The Babe lookt up, and shew'd his face,
    In spite of Darkness it was Day.
It was thy Day, Sweet, and did rise,
Not from the East, but from thy eyes.

Winter chid the world, and sent
    The angry North to wage his warres:
The North forgot his fierce intent,
    And left perfumes instead of scarres:
By those sweet Eyes persuasive powers,
Where he meant frosts, he scattered Flowers.

We saw thee in thy Balmy Nest,
    Bright Dawne of our *Eternall Day*;
We saw thine Eyes break from the East,
    And trace the trembling shades away:
We saw thee (and we blest the sight)
We saw thee by thine own sweet Light.

Wellcome, all Wonders in one sight!
    Eternity, shut in a span.
Summer in winter, Day in Night,
    Heaven in earth and God in Man.
Great little one, whose glorious Birth,
Lifts Earth to Heaven, stoops heaven to earth.

RICHARD CRASHAW (1613?–1649)

The Nativity. *Edward Burne-Jones*

Lord, it belongs not to my care

Lord, it belongs not to my care
   Whether I die or live;
To love and serve thee is my share,
   And this thy grace must give.

If life be long, I will be glad,
   That I may long obey;
If short, yet why should I be sad
   To end my little day?

Christ leads me through no darker rooms
   Than he went through before;
He that into God's kingdom comes
   Must enter by this door.

Come, Lord, when grace hath made me meet
   Thy blessed face to see:
For if thy work on earth be sweet,
   What will thy glory be!

Then I shall end my sad complaints
   And weary, sinful days,
And join with the triumphant Saints
   That sing my Saviour's praise.

My knowledge of that life is small,
   The eye of faith is dim;
But 'tis enough that Christ knows all,
   And I shall be with him.

RICHARD BAXTER (1615–1691)

A Psalm of Praise

Ye holy angels bright,
    Which stand before God's throne,
And dwell in glorious light,
    Praise ye the Lord each one!
      You there so nigh
    Fitter than we
    Dark sinners be,
      For things so high.

You blessed souls at rest,
    Who see your Saviour's face,
Whose glory, e'en the least,
    Is far above our grace.
      God's praises sound,
    As in his sight
    With sweet delight
      You do abound.

Sing forth Jehova's praise,
    Ye saints that on him call!
Magnify him always
    His holy churches all!
      In him rejoice,
    And there proclaim
    His holy name
      With sounding voice.

My soul bear thou thy part,
    Triumph in God above!
With a well-tuned heart,
    Sing thou the songs of love!
      Thou art his own,
    Whose precious blood
      Shed for thy good
    His love made known.

RICHARD BAXTER (1615–1691)

Long did I toil

Long did I toil, and knew no earthly rest,
　Far did I rove, and found no certain home;
At last I sought them in his sheltering breast,
　Who opes his arms, and bids the weary come:
With him I found a home, a rest divine,
And I since then am his, and he is mine.

The good I have is from his stores supplied,
　The ill is only what he deems the best;
He for my Friend, I'm rich with nought beside,
　And poor without him, though of all possessed:
Changes may come, I take, or I resign,
Content, while I am his, while he is mine.

Whate'er may change, in him no change is seen,
　A glorious Sun that wanes not nor declines,
Above the clouds and storms he walks serene,
　And on his people's inward darkness shines:
All may depart, I fret not, nor repine,
While I my Saviour's am, while he is mine.

While here, alas! I know but half his love,
　But half discern him, and but half adore;
But when I meet him in the realms above
　I hope to love him better, praise him more,
And feel, and tell, amid the choir divine,
How fully I am his, and he is mine.

JOHN QUARLES (1624–1665)
　and H F LYTE (1793–1847)

Who would true valour see

Who would true valour see,
    Let him come hither;
One here will constant be,
    Come wind, come weather.
There's no discouragement
Shall make him once relent,
His first avow'd intent
    To be a pilgrim.

Who so beset him round
    With dismal stories,
Do but themselves confound,
    His strength the more is;
No lion can him fright,
He'll with a giant fight;
But he will have a right
    To be a pilgrim.

Hobgoblin nor foul fiend
    Can daunt his spirit;
He knows he at the end
    Shall life inherit.
Then fancies fly away,
He'll fear not what men say;
He'll labour night and day
    To be a pilgrim.

JOHN BUNYAN (1628–1688)

Creator Spirit, by whose aid

Creator Spirit, by whose aid
The world's foundations first were laid,
Come, visit every pious mind;
Come, pour thy joys on human kind;
From sin and sorrow set us free,
And make thy temples worthy thee.

O Source of uncreated light,
The Father's promised Paraclete,
Thrice holy Fount, thrice holy Fire,
Our hearts with heavenly love inspire;
Come, and thy sacred unction bring
To sanctify us while we sing.

Plenteous of grace, descend from high
Rich in thy sevenfold energy;
Make us eternal truths receive,
And practise all that we believe;
Give us thyself, that we may see
The Father and the Son by thee.

Immortal honour, endless fame,
Attend the almighty Father's name;
The Saviour Son be glorified,
Who for lost man's redemption died;
And equal adoration be,
Eternal Paraclete, to thee.

JOHN DRYDEN (1631–1701)
    (*After* Veni, Creator Spiritus)

The Crucifixion. *Anonymous*

Awake, my soul, and with the sun

Awake, my soul, and with the sun
Thy daily stage of duty run;
Shake off dull sloth, and joyful rise
To pay thy morning sacrifice.

Redeem thy mis-spent time that's past
Live this day as if 'twere thy last:
Improve thy talent with due care;
For the great Day thyself prepare.

Let all thy converse be sincere,
Thy conscience as the noon-day clear;
Think how all-seeing God thy ways
And all thy secret thoughts surveys.

By influence of the light Divine
Let thy own light in good works shine;
Reflect all heaven's propitious ways
In ardent love and cheerful praise.

Wake, and lift up thyself, my heart,
And with the Angels bear thy part,
Who all night long unwearied sing
High praise to the eternal King.

Awake, awake, ye heavenly choir,
May your devotion me inspire,
That I like you my age may spend,
Like you may on my God attend.

Glory to thee, who safe hast kept
And hast refreshed me whilst I slept;
Grant, Lord, when I from death shall wake
I may of endless light partake.

Heaven is, dear Lord, where'er thou art,
O never then from me depart;
For to my soul 'tis hell to be
But for one moment void of thee.

Lord, I my vows to thee renew;
Scatter my sins as morning dew;
Guard my first springs of thought and will,
And with thyself my spirit fill.

Direct, control, suggest, this day
All I design, or do, or say;
That all my powers, with all their might,
In thy sole glory may unite.

Praise God, from whom all blessings flow,
Praise him, all creatures here below,
Praise him above, ye heavenly host,
Praise Father, Son, and Holy Ghost.

BISHOP THOMAS KEN (1637–1711)

A Hymn for Christmas Day

Christians, awake, salute the happy morn
Whereon the Saviour of the world was born;
Rise, to adore the Mystery of Love,
Which hosts of Angels chanted from above;
With them the joyful tidings first begun
Of God incarnate and the Virgin's Son:

Then to the watchful shepherds it was told,
Who heard the angelic herald's voice: 'Behold!
I bring good tidings of a Saviour's birth
To you, and all the nations upon earth;
This day hath God fulfilled his promised word;
This day is born a Saviour, Christ, the Lord.'

He spake, and straightway the celestial choir
In hymns of joy, unknown before, conspire;
The praises of redeeming Love they sung,
And heaven's whole orb with Alleluyas rung:
God's highest glory was their anthem still;
Peace upon earth, and mutual good will.

To Bethlehem straight the enlightened shepherds ran,
To see the wonder God had wrought for man;
And found, with Joseph and the blessèd Maid,
Her Son, the Saviour, in a manger laid.
Amazed the wondrous story they proclaim,
The first apostles of his infant fame.

Like Mary, let us ponder in our mind
God's wondrous love in saving lost mankind;
Trace we the Babe, who hath retrieved our loss,
From his poor manger to his bitter cross;
Treading his steps, assisted by his grace,
Till man's first heavenly state again takes place.

JOHN BYROM (1692–1763)

The Magi. *Designed by Sir Edmund Burne-Jones*

Has vidras laudes qui sacra virgine gaudes
Et venerando piam studeas laudare mariam
Virginis intacte dum veneris ante figuram
Pretereunde cave ne taceatur ave
Invenies venia sic salutando mariam. Salve
Alve virgo virginum stella ma
tutina. Sordidorum criminum
vera medicina. Consolatrix lpim
qui sunt in ruina. Precibus pre
sanctum mater et melina. regina
egina virginatum virgo puellaris
Pepedit filium mater singularis
Sacratum palacium di convocaris.

God, that madest earth and heaven

God, that madest earth and heaven,
    Darkness and light;
Who the day for toil hast given,
    For rest the night;
May thine Angel-guards defend us,
Slumber sweet thy mercy send us,
Holy dreams and hopes attend us,
    This livelong night.

Guard us waking, guard us sleeping;
    And, when we die,
May we in thy mighty keeping
    All peaceful lie:
When the last dread call shall wake us,
Do not thou our God forsake us,
But to reign in glory take us
    With thee on high.

BISHOP ROBERT HEBER (1783–1826)
and ARCHBISHOP RICHARD WHATELY (1787–1863)

Virgin and Child. *From a fifteenth century illuminated manuscript.*

Glory to thee, my God, this night

Glory to thee, my God, this night
For all the blessings of the light;
Keep me, O keep me, King of kings,
Beneath thy own almighty wings.

Forgive me, Lord, for thy dear Son,
The ill that I this day have done,
That with the world, myself, and thee,
I, ere I sleep, at peace may be.

Teach me to live, that I may dread
The grave as little as my bed;
Teach me to die, that so I may
Rise glorious at the awful day.

O may my soul on thee repose,
And with sweet sleep mine eyelids close,
Sleep that may me more vigorous make
To serve my God when I awake.

When in the night I sleepless lie,
My soul with heavenly thoughts supply;
Let no ill dreams disturb my rest,
No powers of darkness me molest.

You, my blest guardian, whilst I sleep
Close to my bed your vigils keep;
Divine love into me instil,
Stop all the avenues of ill.

Praise God, from whom all blessings flow,
Praise him, all creatures here below,
Praise him above, ye heavenly host,
Praise Father, Son, and Holy Ghost.

BISHOP THOMAS KEN (1637–1711)

Through all the changing scenes of life

Through all the changing scenes of life,
  In trouble and in joy,
The praises of my God shall still
  My heart and tongue employ.

O magnify the Lord with me,
  With me exalt his name;
When in distress to him I called,
  He to my rescue came.

The hosts of God encamped around
  The dwellings of the just;
Deliverance he affords to all
  Who on his succour trust.

O make but trial of his love,
  Experience will decide
How blest they are, and only they,
  Who in his truth confide.

Fear him, ye saints, and you will then
  Have nothing else to fear;
Make you his service your delight,
  Your wants shall be his care.

To Father, Son, and Holy Ghost,
  The God whom we adore,
Be glory, as it was, is now,
  And shall be evermore.

NAHUM TATE (1652–1715)
and NICHOLAS BRADY (1659–1726)
  (after Psalm 34)

As pants the hart

As pants the hart for cooling streams
    When heated in the chase,
So longs my soul, O God, for thee,
    And thy refreshing grace.

For thee, my God, the living God,
    My thirsty soul doth pine:
O when shall I behold thy face,
    Thou Majesty Divine!

Why restless, why cast down, my soul?
    Hope still, and thou shalt sing
The praise of him who is thy God,
    Thy health's eternal spring.

To Father, Son, and Holy Ghost,
    The God whom we adore,
Be glory, as it was, is now,
    And shall be evermore.

NAHUM TATE (1652–1715)
and NICHOLAS BRADY (1659–1726)
    (after Psalm 42)

From the 'Wilton Diptych'

The Confirmation of faith

The spacious firmament on high,
With all the blue ethereal sky,
And spangled heavens, a shining frame,
Their great Original proclaim.
The unwearied sun from day to day
Does his Creator's power display,
And publishes to every land
The works of an Almighty hand.

Soon as the evening shades prevail,
The moon takes up the wondrous tale;
And nightly to the listening earth,
Repeats the story of her birth;
Whilst all the stars that round her burn,
And all the planets in their turn,
Confirm the tidings, as they roll,
And spread the truth from pole to pole.

What though in solemn silence all
Move round the dark terrestrial ball;
What though nor real voice nor sound
Amid their radiant orbs be found?
In reason's ear they all rejoice,
And utter forth a glorious voice;
For ever singing as they shine,
'The hand that made us is divine.'

JOSEPH ADDISON (1672–1719)

The Angel Standing in the Sun. *J M W Turner*

When all thy mercies, O my God

When all thy mercies, O my God,
  My rising soul surveys,
Transported with the view, I'm lost
  In wonder, love, and praise.

Unnumbered comforts to my soul
  Thy tender care bestowed,
Before my infant heart conceived
  From whom those comforts flowed.

When in the slippery paths of youth
  With heedless steps I ran,
Thine arms unseen conveyed me safe,
  And led me up to man.

When worn with sickness oft hast thou
  With health renewed my face;
And when in sins and sorrows sunk,
  Revived my soul with grace.

Through every period of my life
  Thy goodness I'll pursue,
And after death in distant worlds
  The glorious theme renew.

Through all eternity to thee
  A joyful song I'll raise;
For O! eternity's too short
  To utter all thy praise.

JOSEPH ADDISON (1672–1719)

There is a land of pure delight

There is a land of pure delight
    Where saints immortal reign;
Infinite day excludes the night,
    And pleasures banish pain.

There everlasting spring abides,
    And never-withering flowers:
Death like a narrow sea divides
    This heavenly land from ours.

Sweet fields beyond the swelling flood
    Stand dressed in living green:
So to the Jews old Canaan stood,
    While Jordan rolled between.

But timorous mortals start and shrink
    To cross this narrow sea,
And linger shivering on the brink
    And fear to launch away.

O could we make our doubts remove,
    These gloomy doubts that rise,
And see the Canaan that we love,
    With unbeclouded eyes.

Could we but climb where Moses stood,
    And view the landscape o'er,
Not Jordan's stream, nor Death's cold flood,
    Should fright us from the shore.

ISAAC WATTS (1674–1748)

Our God, our help in ages past

Our God, our help in ages past,
    Our hope for years to come,
Our shelter from the stormy blast,
    And our eternal home.

Under the shadow of thy throne
    Thy saints have dwelt secure;
Sufficient is thine arm alone,
    And our defence is sure.

Before the hills in order stood,
    Or earth received her frame,
From everlasting thou art God,
    To endless years the same.

Thy Word commands our flesh to dust,
    'Return, ye sons of men':
All nations rose from earth at first,
    And turn to earth again.

A thousand ages in thy sight
    Are like an evening gone;
Short as the watch that ends the night
    Before the rising sun.

The busy tribes of flesh and blood
    With all their lives and cares
Are carried downwards by thy flood
    And lost in following years.

Time like an ever-rolling stream
    Bears all its sons away;
They fly forgotten as a dream
    Dies at the opening day.

Like flowery fields the nations stand
    Pleased with the morning light;
The flowers beneath the mower's hand
    Lie withering ere 'tis night.

Our God, our help in ages past,
    Our hope for years to come,
Be thou our guard while troubles last,
    And our eternal home.

ISAAC WATTS (1674–1748)

Jesus shall reign where'er the sun

Jesus shall reign where'er the sun
Does his successive journeys run;
His kingdom stretch from shore to shore,
Till moons shall wax and wane no more.

People and realms of every tongue
Dwell on his love with sweetest song,
And infant voices shall proclaim
Their early blessings on his name.

Blessings abound where'er he reigns;
The prisoner leaps to lose his chains;
The weary find eternal rest,
And all the sons of want are blest.

Let every creature rise and bring
Peculiar honours to our King;
Angels descend with songs again,
And earth repeat the long amen.

ISAAC WATTS (1674–1748)

Hark! the herald Angels sing

Hark! the herald Angels sing
Glory to the new-born King;
Peace on earth and mercy mild,
God and sinners reconciled:
Joyful all ye nations rise,
Join the triumph of the skies,
With the angelic host proclaim,
Christ is born in Bethlehem.

Hark! the herald Angels sing
Glory to the new-born King.

Christ, by highest heaven adored,
Christ, the everlasting Lord,
Late in time behold him come
Offspring of a Virgin's womb!
Veiled in flesh the Godhead see,
Hail the incarnate Deity!
Pleased as man with man to dwell,
Jesus, our Emmanuel.

Hail the heaven-born Prince of peace!
Hail the Sun of Righteousness!
Light and life to all he brings,
Risen with healing in his wings;
Mild he lays his glory by,
Born that man no more may die,
Born to raise the sons of earth,
Born to give them second birth.

CHARLES WESLEY (1707–1788)
and others

Angels. *Walter Crane*

Jesu, Lover of my soul

Jesu, Lover of my soul,
   Let me to thy bosom fly,
While the nearer waters roll,
   While the tempest still is high:
Hide me, O my Saviour, hide,
   Till the storm of life is past;
Safe into the haven guide,
   O receive my soul at last.

Other refuge have I none;
   Hangs my helpless soul on thee;
Leave, ah! leave me not alone,
   Still support and comfort me.
All my trust on thee is stayed,
   All my help from thee I bring;
Cover my defenceless head
   With the shadow of thy wing.

Thou, O Christ, art all I want;
   More than all in thee I find:
Raise the fallen, cheer the faint,
   Heal the sick, and lead the blind.
Just and holy is thy name;
   I am all unrighteousness;
False and full of sin I am,
   Thou art full of truth and grace.

Plenteous grace with thee is found,
   Grace to cover all my sin;
Let the healing streams abound;
   Make and keep me pure within.
Thou of life the fountain art;
   Freely let me take of thee;
Spring thou up within my heart,
   Rise to all eternity.

CHARLES WESLEY (1707–1788)

The Light of the World. *W Holman Hunt*

O for a thousand tongues to sing

O for a thousand tongues to sing
   My dear Redeemer's praise,
The glories of my God and King,
   The triumphs of his grace!

Jesus – the name that charms our fears,
   That bids our sorrows cease;
'Tis music in the sinner's ears,
   'Tis life, and health, and peace.

He breaks the power of cancelled sin,
   He sets the prisoner free;
His Blood can make the foulest clean;
   His Blood availed for me.

He speaks; – and, listening to his voice,
   New life the dead receive,
The mournful broken hearts rejoice,
   The humble poor believe.

Hear him, ye deaf; his praise, ye dumb,
   Your loosened tongues employ;
Ye blind, behold your Saviour come;
   And leap, ye lame, for joy!

My gracious Master and my God,
   Assist me to proclaim
And spread through all the earth abroad
   The honours of thy name.

CHARLES WESLEY (1707–1788)

O for a heart to praise my God

O for a heart to praise my God,
   A heart from sin set free;
A heart that always feels thy Blood
   So freely spilt for me:

A heart resigned, submissive, meek,
   My dear Redeemer's throne;
Where only Christ is heard to speak,
   Where Jesus reigns alone:

A humble, lowly, contrite heart,
   Believing, true, and clean,
Which neither life nor death can part
   From him that dwells within:

A heart in every thought renewed,
   And full of love divine;
Perfect, and right, and pure, and good,
   A copy, Lord, of thine.

My heart, thou know'st, can never rest
   Till thou create my peace;
Till of mine Eden repossest,
   From self, and sin, I cease.

Thy nature, gracious Lord, impart,
   Come quickly from above;
Write thy new name upon my heart,
   Thy new best name of love.

CHARLES WESLEY (1707–1788)

Retirement

Far from the world, O Lord, I flee,
   From strife and tumult far;
From scenes, where Satan wages still
   His most successful war.

The calm retreat, the silent shade,
   With pray'r and praise agree;
And seem by thy sweet bounty made,
   For those who follow thee.

There if thy Spirit touch the soul,
   And grace her mean abode;
Oh with what peace, and joy, and love
   She communes with her God!

There like the nightingale she pours
   Her solitary lays;
Nor asks a witness of her song,
   Nor thirsts for human praise.

Author and Guardian of my life,
   Sweet source of light divine;
And (all harmonious names in one)
   My Saviour; thou art mine!

What thanks I owe thee, and what love,
   A boundless, endless store,
Shall echo thro' the realms above,
   When time shall be no more.

WILLIAM COWPER (1731–1800)

Glorious things of thee are spoken

Glorious things of thee are spoken,
   Sion, city of our God!
He whose word cannot be broken
   Formed thee for his own abode:
On the Rock of Ages founded,
   What can shake thy sure repose?
With salvation's walls surrounded,
   Thou may'st smile at all thy foes.

See, the streams of living waters,
   Springing from eternal love,
Well supply thy sons and daughters,
   And all fear of want remove:
Who can faint while such a river
   Ever flows their thirst to assuage?
Grace, which like the Lord the Giver,
   Never fails from age to age.

Saviour, if of Sion's city
   I, through grace, a member am,
Let the world deride or pity,
   I will glory in thy name:
Fading is the worldling's pleasure,
   All his boasted pomp and show;
Solid joys and lasting treasure
   None but Sion's children know.

JOHN NEWTON (1725–1807)

Durham
Thomas Bewick

Hark, my soul! it is the Lord

Hark, my soul! it is the Lord;
'Tis thy Saviour, hear his word;
Jesus speaks, and speaks to thee:
'Say, poor sinner, lov'st thou me?

'I delivered thee when bound,
And, when wounded, healed thy wound;
Sought thee wandering, set thee right,
Turned thy darkness into light.

'Can a woman's tender care
Cease towards the child she bare?
Yes, she may forgetful be,
Yet will I remember thee.

'Mine is an unchanging love,
Higher than the heights above,
Deeper than the depths beneath,
Free and faithful, strong as death.

'Thou shalt see my glory soon,
When the work of grace is done;
Partner of my throne shalt be;
Say, poor sinner, lov'st thou me?'

Lord, it is my chief complaint
That my love is weak and faint;
Yet I love thee, and adore;
O for grace to love thee more!

WILLIAM COWPER (1731–1800)

God moves in a mysterious way

God moves in a mysterious way
   His wonders to perform;
He plants his footsteps in the sea,
   And rides upon the storm.

Deep in unfathomable mines
   Of never-failing skill
He treasures up his bright designs,
   And works his sovereign will.

Ye fearful saints, fresh courage take,
   The clouds ye so much dread
Are big with mercy, and shall break
   In blessings on your head.

Judge not the Lord by feeble sense,
   But trust him for his grace;
Behind a frowning providence
   He hides a smiling face.

His purposes will ripen fast,
   Unfolding every hour;
The bud may have a bitter taste,
   But sweet will be the flower.

Blind unbelief is sure to err,
   And scan his work in vain;
God is his own interpreter,
   And he will make it plain.

WILLIAM COWPER (1731–1800)

O for a closer walk with God

O for a closer walk with God,
   A calm and heavenly frame;
A light to shine upon the road
   That leads me to the Lamb!

Return, O holy Dove, return,
   Sweet messenger of rest;
I hate the sins that made thee mourn,
   And drove thee from my breast.

The dearest idol I have known,
   Whate'er that idol be,
Help me to tear it from thy throne,
   And worship only thee.

So shall my walk be close with God,
   Calm and serene my frame;
So purer light shall mark the road
   That leads me to the Lamb.

WILLIAM COWPER (1731–1800)

O Thou from whom all goodness flows

O Thou from whom all goodness flows,
  I lift my heart to thee;
In all my sorrows, conflicts, woes,
  Dear Lord, remember me.

When on my poor distressèd heart
  My sins lie heavily,
Thy pardon grant, new peace impart:
  Dear Lord, remember me.

When trials sore obstruct my way,
  And ills I cannot flee,
O let my strength be as my day:
  Dear Lord, remember me.

If, for thy sake, upon my name
  Shame and reproaches be,
All hail reproach and welcome shame:
  Dear Lord, remember me.

If worn with pain, disease, or grief
  This feeble spirit be;
Grant patience, rest, and kind relief:
  Dear Lord, remember me.

And O, when in the hour of death
  I wait thy just decree,
Be this the prayer of my last breath:
  Dear Lord, remember me.

THOMAS HAWEIS (1732–1820)
  and others

The Return Home. *Edward Calvert*

Rock of Ages

Rock of Ages, cleft for me,
Let me hide myself in Thee!
Let the water and the blood
From Thy riven side which flow'd,
Be of sin the double cure,
Cleanse me from its guilt and power.

Not the labours of my hands
Can fulfil Thy law's demands;
Could my zeal no respite know,
Could my tears for ever flow,
All for sin could not atone;
Thou must save, and Thou alone.

Nothing in my hand I bring;
Simply to Thy Cross I cling;
Naked, come to Thee for dress;
Helpless, look to Thee for grace;
Foul, I to the Fountain fly;
Wash me, Saviour, or I die!

While I draw this fleeting breath,
When my eyestrings break in death,
When I soar through tracts unknown,
See Thee on Thy Judgement-throne;
Rock of Ages, cleft for me,
Let me hide myself in Thee!

AUGUSTUS MONTAGUE TOPLADY (1740–1778)

Crucifixion. *Illuminated MS*

Rest on the Flight into Egypt. *Samuel Palmer*

Sweet dreams, form a shade

Sweet dreams, form a shade
O'er my lovely infant's head:
Sweet dreams of pleasant streams
By happy, silent, moony beams.

Sweet sleep, with soft down
Weave thy brows an infant crown.
Sweet sleep, angel mild,
Hover o'er my happy child.

Sleep, sleep, happy child,
All creation slept and smiled;
Sleep, sleep, happy sleep,
While o'er thee thy mother weep.

Sweet babe, in thy face
Holy image I can trace.
Sweet babe, once like thee,
Thy Maker lay, and wept for me.

Wept for me, for thee, for all,
When he was an infant small.
Thou his image ever see,
Heavenly face that smiles on thee.

Smiles on thee, on me, on all;
Who became an infant small.
Infant smiles are his own smiles;
Heaven and earth to peace beguiles.

WILLIAM BLAKE (1757–1827)

To Mercy, Pity, Peace, and Love

To Mercy, Pity, Peace, and Love,
  All pray in their distress,
And to these virtues of delight
  Return their thankfulness.

For Mercy, Pity, Peace, and Love,
  Is God our Father dear;
And Mercy, Pity, Peace, and Love,
  Is Man, his child and care.

For Mercy has a human heart,
  Pity, a human face;
And Love, the human form divine,
  And Peace, the human dress.

Then every man, of every clime,
  That prays in his distress,
Prays to the human form divine:
  Love, Mercy, Pity, Peace.

And all must love the human form,
  In heathen, Turk, or Jew;
Where Mercy, Love, and Pity dwell,
  There God is dwelling too.

WILLIAM BLAKE (1757–1827)

The Angel of the Divine Presence. *William Blake*

Jerusalem

And did those feet in ancient time
   Walk upon England's mountains green?
And was the holy Lamb of God
   On England's pleasant pastures seen?
And did the countenance divine
   Shine forth upon our clouded hills?
And was Jerusalem builded here
   Among those dark satanic mills?

Bring me my bow of burning gold!
   Bring me my arrows of desire!
Bring me my spear! O clouds, unfold!
   Bring me my chariot of fire!
I will not cease from mental fight,
   Nor shall my sword sleep in my hand,
Till we have built Jerusalem
   In England's green and pleasant land.

WILLIAM BLAKE (1757–1827)

Blest are the moments, doubly blest

Blest are the moments, doubly blest,
That, drawn from this one hour of rest,
Are with a ready heart bestowed
Upon the service of our God!

Each field is then a hallowed spot,
An altar is in each man's cot,
A church in every grove that spreads
Its living roof above our heads.

Look up to heaven! the industrious sun
Already half his race hath run;
He cannot halt or go astray,
But our immortal spirits may.

Lord, since his rising in the east,
If we have faltered or transgressed,
Guide, from thy love's abundant source,
What yet remains of this day's course;

Help with thy grace, through life's short day,
Our upward and our downward way;
And glorify for us the west,
When we shall sink to final rest.

WILLIAM WORDSWORTH (1770–1850)

Acts I c.

The head that once was crowned with thorns

The head that once was crowned with thorns
   Is crowned with glory now:
A royal diadem adorns
   The mighty Victor's brow.

The highest place that heaven affords
   Is his, is his by right,
The King of kings and Lord of lords,
   And heaven's eternal Light;

The joy of all who dwell above,
   The joy of all below,
To whom he manifests his love,
   And grants his name to know.

To them the Cross, with all its shame,
   With all its grace is given:
Their name an everlasting name,
   Their joy the joy of heaven.

They suffer with their Lord below,
   They reign with him above,
Their profit and their joy to know
   The mystery of his love.

The Cross he bore is life and health,
   Though shame and death to him;
His people's hope, his people's wealth,
   Their everlasting theme.

THOMAS KELLY (1769–1854)

The Ascension. *William Blake*

O worship the King

O worship the King
  All glorious above;
O gratefully sing
  His power and his love:
Our Shield and Defender,
  The Ancient of days,
Pavilioned in splendour,
  And girded with praise.

O tell of his might,
  O sing of his grace,
Whose robe is the light,
  Whose canopy space.
His chariots of wrath
  The deep thunder-clouds form.
And dark is his path
  On the wings of the storm.

This earth, with its store
  Of wonders untold,
Almighty, thy power
  Hath founded of old;
Hath stablished it fast
  By a changeless decree,
And round it hath cast,
  Like a mantle, the sea.

Thy bountiful care
   What tongue can recite?
It breathes in the air,
   It shines in the light;
It streams from the hills,
   It descends to the plain,
And sweetly distils
   In the dew and the rain.

Frail children of dust,
   And feeble as frail,
In thee do we trust,
   Nor find thee to fail:
Thy mercies how tender!
   How firm to the end!
Our Maker, Defender,
   Redeemer, and Friend.

O measureless Might,
   Ineffable Love,
While Angels delight
   To hymn thee above,
Thy humbler creation,
   Though feeble their lays,
With true adoration
   Shall sing to thy praise.

SIR ROBERT GRANT (1779–1838)

That day of wrath, that dreadful day

That day of wrath, that dreadful day,
When heaven and earth shall pass away,
What power shall be the sinner's stay?
How shall he meet that dreadful day?

When, shrivelling like a parchèd scroll,
The flaming heavens together roll;
When louder yet, and yet more dread,
Swells the high trump that wakes the dead:

O, on that day, that wrathful day,
When man to judgement wakes from clay,
Be thou the trembling sinner's stay,
Though heaven and earth shall pass away!

SIR WALTER SCOTT (1771–1832)

The Last Judgement. *William Blake*

Our blest Redeemer, ere he breathed

Our blest Redeemer, ere he breathed
  His tender last farewell,
A Guide, a Comforter, bequeathed
    With us to dwell.

He came in tongues of living flame,
  To teach, convince, subdue;
All-powerful as the wind he came,
    As viewless too.

He came sweet influence to impart,
  A gracious, willing Guest,
While he can find one humble heart
    Wherein to rest.

And his that gentle voice we hear,
  Soft as the breath of even,
That checks each fault, that calms each fear,
    And speaks of heaven.

And every virtue we possess,
  And every victory won,
And every thought of holiness,
    Are his alone.

Spirit of purity and grace,
  Our weakness, pitying, see:
O make our hearts thy dwelling-place,
    And worthier thee.

HARRIET AUBER (1773–1862)

When wilt thou save the people

When wilt thou save the people O God of mercy when?
The people, Lord, the people,
Not thrones and crowns, but men!
Flowers of thy heart, O God, are they;
Let them not pass, like weeds, away.
Their heritage a sunless day.
God save the people!

Shall crime bring crime for ever,
Strength aiding still the strong?
Is it thy will, O Father,
That man shall toil for wrong?
'No', say thy mountains; 'No', thy skies;
Man's clouded sun shall brightly rise,
And songs be heard instead of sighs.
God save the people!

When wilt thou save the people?
O God of mercy, when?
The people, Lord, the people,
Not thrones and crowns, but men!
God save the people; thine they are,
Thy children, as thy Angels fair;
From vice, oppression, and despair,
God save the people!

EBENEZER ELLIOTT (1781–1840)

Brightest and best of the sons of the morning

Brightest and best of the sons of the morning,
  Dawn on our darkness and lend us thine aid;
Star of the East, the horizon adorning,
  Guide where our infant Redeemer is laid.

Cold on his cradle the dew-drops are shining,
  Low lies his head with the beasts of the stall:
Angels adore him in slumber reclining,
  Maker and Monarch and Saviour of all.

Say, shall we yield him, in costly devotion,
  Odours of Edom and offerings divine?
Gems of the mountain and pearls of the ocean,
  Myrrh from the forest or gold from the mine?

Vainly we offer each ample oblation,
  Vainly with gifts would his favour secure;
Richer by far is the heart's adoration,
  Dearer to God are the prayers of the poor.

Brightest and best of the sons of the morning,
  Dawn on our darkness and lend us thine aid;
Star of the East, the horizon adorning,
  Guide where our infant Redeemer is laid.

BISHOP ROBERT HEBER (1783–1826)

The Spirit of Christianity. *G F Watts*

Lord, I would own thy tender care

Lord, I would own thy tender care,
   And all thy love to me;
The food I eat, the clothes I wear,
   Are all bestowed by thee.

'Tis thou preservest me from death
   And dangers every hour;
I cannot draw another breath
   Unless thou give me power.

Kind Angels guard me every night,
   As round my bed they stay;
Nor am I absent from thy sight
   In darkness or by day.

My health and friends and parents dear
   To me by God are given;
I have not any blessing here
   But what is sent from heaven.

Such goodness, Lord, and constant care,
   A child can ne'er repay;
But may it be my daily prayer
   To love thee and obey.

JANE TAYLOR (1783–1824)

New every morning is the love

New every morning is the love
Our wakening and uprising prove;
Through sleep and darkness safely brought,
Restored to life, and power, and thought.

New mercies, each returning day,
Hover around us while we pray;
New perils past, new sins forgiven,
New thoughts of God, new hopes of heaven.

If on our daily course our mind
Be set to hallow all we find,
New treasures still, of countless price,
God will provide for sacrifice.

Old friends, old scenes, will lovelier be,
As more of heaven in each we see;
Some softening gleam of love and prayer
Shall dawn on every cross and care.

We need not bid, for cloistered cell,
Our neighbour and our work farewell,
Nor strive to wind ourselves too high
For sinful man beneath the sky:

The trivial round, the common task,
Would furnish all we ought to ask, –
Room to deny ourselves, a road
To bring us daily nearer God.

Only, O Lord, in thy dear love
Fit us for perfect rest above;
And help us this and every day
To live more nearly as we pray.

JOHN KEBLE (1792–1866)

There is a book who runs may read

There is a book who runs may read,
  Which heavenly truth imparts,
And all the lore its scholars need,
  Pure eyes and Christian hearts.

The works of God above, below,
  Within us and around,
Are pages in that book, to show
  How God himself is found.

The glorious sky, embracing all,
  Is like the Maker's love,
Wherewith encompassed, great and small
  In peace and order move.

The moon above, the Church below,
  A wondrous race they run;
But all their radiance, all their glow,
  Each borrows of its sun.

The Saviour lends the light and heat
  That crowns his holy hill;
The Saints, like stars, around his seat
  Perform their courses still.

The Saints above are stars in heaven –
  What are the saints on earth?
Like trees they stand whom God has given,
  Our Eden's happy birth.

Faith is their fixed unswerving root,
  Hope their unfading flower,
Fair deeds of charity their fruit,
  The glory of their bower.

The dew of heaven is like thy grace,
　　It steals in silence down;
But where it lights, the favoured place,
　　By richest fruits is known.

One name, above all glorious names,
　　With its ten thousand tongues,
The everlasting sea proclaims,
　　Echoing angelic songs.

The raging fire, the roaring wind,
　　Thy boundless power display;
But in the gentler breeze we find
　　Thy Spirit's viewless way.

Two worlds are ours: 'tis only sin
　　Forbids us to descry
The mystic heaven and earth within,
　　Plain as the sea and sky.

Thou, who hast given me eyes to see
　　And love this sight so fair,
Give me a heart to find out thee,
　　And read thee everywhere.

JOHN KEBLE (1792–1866)

Thomas Bewick

Sun of my soul, thou Saviour dear

Sun of my soul, thou Saviour dear,
It is not night if thou be near:
O may no earth-born cloud arise
To hide thee from thy servant's eyes.

When the soft dews of kindly sleep
My wearied eyelids gently steep,
Be my last thought, how sweet to rest
For ever on my Saviour's breast.

Abide with me from morn till eve,
For without thee I cannot live;
Abide with me when night is nigh,
For without thee I dare not die.

If some poor wand'ring child of thine
Have spurned to-day the voice divine,
Now, Lord, the gracious work begin;
Let him no more lie down in sin.

Watch by the sick; enrich the poor
With blessings from thy boundless store;
Be every mourner's sleep to-night
Like infant's slumbers, pure and light.

Come near and bless us when we wake,
Ere through the world our way we take;
Till in the ocean of thy love
We lose ourselves in heaven above.

JOHN KEBLE (1792–1866)

Abide with me

Abide with me; fast falls the eventide;
The darkness deepens; Lord, with me abide!
When other helpers fail, and comforts flee,
Help of the helpless, O abide with me.

Swift to its close ebbs out life's little day;
Earth's joys grow dim, its glories pass away;
Change and decay in all around I see;
O thou who changest not, abide with me.

I need thy presence every passing hour;
What but thy grace can foil the tempter's power?
Who like thyself my guide and stay can be?
Through cloud and sunshine, O abide with me.

I fear no foe with thee at hand to bless;
Ills have no weight, and tears no bitterness.
Where is death's sting? where, grave, thy victory?
I triumph still, if thou abide with me.

Hold thou thy Cross before my closing eyes;
Shine through the gloom, and point me to the skies;
Heaven's morning breaks, and earth's vain shadows flee;
In life, in death, O Lord, abide with me!

H F LYTE (1793–1847)

Lead, kindly Light

Lead, kindly Light, amid the encircling gloom,
    Lead thou me on;
The night is dark, and I am far from home,
    Lead thou me on.
Keep thou my feet; I do not ask to see
The distant scene; one step enough for me.

I was not ever thus, nor prayed that thou
    Shouldst lead me on;
I loved to choose and see my path; but now
    Lead thou me on.
I loved the garish day, and, spite of fears,
Pride ruled my will: remember not past years.

So long thy power hath blest me, sure it still
    Will lead me on
O'er moor and fen, o'er crag and torrent, till
    The night is gone,
And with the morn those Angel faces smile,
Which I have loved long since, and lost awhile.

CARDINAL J H NEWMAN (1801–1890)

Tattershall. *From an etching by F L Griggs*

A few more years shall roll

A few more years shall roll,
A few more seasons come,
And we shall be with those that rest
In peace beyond the tomb.
Then, O my Lord, prepare
My soul for that great day;
O wash me in thy precious Blood,
And take my sins away.

A few more suns shall set
O'er these dark hills of time,
And we shall be where suns are not,
A far serener clime.
Then, O my Lord, prepare
My soul for that blest day;
O wash me in thy precious Blood,
And take my sins away.

A few more storms shall beat
On this wild rocky shore,
And we shall be where tempests cease,
And surges swell no more.
Then, O my Lord, prepare
My soul for that calm day;
O wash me in thy precious Blood,
And take my sins away.

A few more struggles here,
A few more partings o'er,
A few more toils, a few more tears,
And we shall weep no more.
Then, O my Lord, prepare
My soul for that blest day;
O wash me in thy precious Blood,
And take my sins away.

'Tis but a little while
And he shall come again,
Who died that we might live, who lives
That we with him may reign.
Then, O my Lord, prepare
My soul for that glad day;
O wash me in thy precious Blood,
And take my sins away.

HORATIUS BONAR (1808–1889)

Strong Son of God

Strong Son of God, immortal Love,
  Whom we, that have not seen thy face,
  By faith, and faith alone, embrace,
Believing where we cannot prove:

Thou wilt not leave us in the dust;
  Thou madest man, he knows not why;
  He thinks he was not made to die:
And thou hast made him, thou art just.

Thou seemest human and divine,
  The highest, holiest manhood thou:
  Our wills are ours, we know not how;
Our wills are ours, to make them thine.

Our little systems have their day;
  They have their day and cease to be:
  They are but broken lights of thee,
And thou, O Lord, art more than they.

ALFRED, LORD TENNYSON (1809–1892)

The Annunciation. *Illuminated MS*

O worship the Lord in the beauty of holiness!

O worship the Lord in the beauty of holiness!
  Bow down before him, his glory proclaim;
With gold of obedience, and incense of lowliness,
  Kneel and adore him, the Lord is his name!

Low at his feet lay thy burden of carefulness,
  High on his heart he will bear it for thee,
Comfort thy sorrows, and answer thy prayerfulness,
  Guiding thy steps as may best for thee be.

Fear not to enter his courts in the slenderness
  Of the poor wealth thou wouldst reckon as thine:
Truth in its beauty, and love in its tenderness,
  These are the offerings to lay on his shrine.

These, though we bring them in trembling and fearfulness,
  He will accept for the name that is dear;
Mornings of joy give for evenings of tearfulness,
  Trust for our trembling and hope for our fear.

O worship the Lord in the beauty of holiness!
  Bow down before him, his glory proclaim;
With gold of obedience, and incense of lowliness,
  Kneel and adore him, the Lord is his name!

J S B MONSELL (1811–1875)
(*from the medieval German*)

All things bright and beautiful

All things bright and beautiful,
　All creatures great and small,
All things wise and wonderful,
　The Lord God made them all.

Each little flower that opens,
　Each little bird that sings,
He made their glowing colours,
　He made their tiny wings.

The rich man in his castle,
　The poor man at his gate,
God made them, high or lowly,
　And order'd their estate.

The purple headed mountain,
　The river running by,
The sunset and the morning,
　That brightens up the sky.

The cold wind in the winter,
　The pleasant summer sun,
The ripe fruits in the garden,
　He made them every one.

The tall trees in the greenwood,
　The meadows for our play,
The rushes by the water,
　To gather every day.

He gave us eyes to see them,
　And lips that we might tell
How great is God Almighty,
　Who has made all things well.

MRS C F ALEXANDER (1818–1895)

The Early Ploughman. *Samuel Palmer*

There is a green hill far away

There is a green hill far away,
 Without a city wall,
Where the dear Lord was crucified
 Who died to save us all.

We may not know, we cannot tell,
 What pains he had to bear,
But we believe it was for us
 He hung and suffered there.

He died that we might be forgiven,
 He died to make us good;
That we might go at last to heaven,
 Saved by his precious Blood.

There was no other good enough
 To pay the price of sin;
He only could unlock the gate
 Of heaven, and let us in.

O, dearly, dearly has he loved,
 And we must love him too,
And trust in his redeeming Blood.
 And try his works to do.

MRS C F ALEXANDER (1818–1895)

Art thou weary, art thou languid

Art thou weary, art thou languid,
  Art thou sore distrest?
'Come to me,' saith One, 'and coming
      Be at rest!'

Hath he marks to lead me to him,
  If he be my Guide?
'In his feet and hands are wound-prints,
      And his side.'

Is there diadem as Monarch
  That his brow adorns?
'Yea, a crown, in very surety,
      But of thorns.'

If I find him, if I follow,
  What his guerdon here?
'Many a sorrow, many a labour,
      Many a tear.'

If I still hold closely to him,
  What hath he at last?
'Sorrow vanquished, labour ended,
      Jordan past.'

If I ask him to receive me,
  Will he say me nay?
'Not till earth, and not till heaven
      Pass away.'

Finding, following, keeping, struggling,
  Is he sure to bless?
'Angels, Martyrs, Prophets, Virgins,
      Answer, Yes!'

J M NEALE (1818–1866)

Christian, dost thou see them

Christian, dost thou see them
　　On the holy ground,
How the troops of Midian
　　Prowl and prowl around?
Christian, up and smite them,
　　Counting gain but loss;
Smite them by the merit
　　Of the holy Cross.

Christian, dost thou feel them,
　　How they work within,
Striving, tempting, luring,
　　Goading into sin?
Christian, never tremble;
　　Never be down-cast;
Smite them by the virtue
　　Of the Lenten fast.

Christian, dost thou hear them,
　　How they speak thee fair?
'Always fast and vigil?
　　Always watch and prayer?'
Christian, answer boldly,
　　'While I breathe, I pray':
Peace shall follow battle,
　　Night shall end in day.

'Well I know thy trouble,
　　O my servant true;
Thou art very weary, –
　　I was weary too;
But that toil shall make thee
　　Some day all mine own, –
But the end of sorrow
　　Shall be near my throne.'

J M NEALE (1818–1866)
(from the Greek)

'Tis winter now; the fallen snow

'Tis winter now; the fallen snow
Has left the heavens all coldly clear;
Through leafless boughs the sharp winds blow,
And all the earth lies dead and drear.

And yet God's love is not withdrawn;
His life within the keen air breathes;
His beauty paints the crimson dawn,
And clothes the boughs with glittering wreaths.

And though abroad the sharp winds blow,
And skies are chill, and frosts are keen,
Home closer draws her circle now,
And warmer glows her light within.

O God! who giv'st the winter's cold,
As well as summer's joyous rays,
Us warmly in thy love enfold,
And keep us through life's wintry days.

SAMUEL LONGFELLOW (1819–1892)

For all the Saints

For all the Saints who from their labours rest,
Who thee by faith before the world confest,
Thy name, O Jesu, be for ever blest.
                                    Alleluya!

Thou wast their Rock, their Fortress, and their Might;
Thou, Lord, their Captain in the well-fought fight;
Thou in the darkness drear their one true Light.

O may thy soldiers, faithful, true, and bold,
Fight as the Saints who nobly fought of old,
And win, with them, the victor's crown of gold.

O blest communion! fellowship divine!
We feebly struggle, they in glory shine;
Yet all are one in thee, for all are thine.

And when the strife is fierce, the warfare long
Steals on the ear the distant triumph-song,
And hearts are brave again, and arms are strong.

The golden evening brightens in the west;
Soon, soon to faithful warriors cometh rest:
Sweet is the calm of Paradise the blest.

But lo! there breaks a yet more glorious day;
The Saints triumphant rise in bright array:
The King of glory passes on his way.

From earth's wide bounds, from ocean's farthest coast,
Through gates of pearl streams in the countless host,
Singing to Father, Son, and Holy Ghost.

BISHOP W W HOW (1823–1897)

Hallelujah. *Arthur Hughes*

In the bleak mid-winter

In the bleak mid-winter
   Frosty wind made moan,
Earth stood hard as iron,
   Water like a stone;
Snow had fallen, snow on snow,
   Snow on snow,
In the bleak mid-winter,
   Long ago.

Our God, heaven cannot hold him
   Nor earth sustain;
Heaven and earth shall flee away
   When he comes to reign:
In the bleak mid-winter
   A stable-place sufficed
The Lord God Almighty
   Jesus Christ.

Enough for him, whom Cherubim
   Worship night and day,
A breastful of milk,
   And a mangerful of hay;
Enough for him, whom Angels
   Fall down before,
The ox and ass and camel
   Which adore.

Angels and Archangels
  May have gathered there,
Cherubim and Seraphim
  Thronged the air –
But only his mother
  In her maiden bliss
Worshipped the Beloved
  With a kiss.

What can I give him
  Poor as I am?
If I were a shepherd
  I would bring a lamb;
If I were a wise man
  I would do my part;
Yet what can I give him –
  Give my heart.

CHRISTINA ROSSETTI (1830–1894)

OVERLEAF Bethlehem. *From an engraving after J M W Turner by W Finden*

What are these that glow from afar

What are these that glow from afar,
These that lean over the golden bar,
Strong as the lion, pure as the dove,
With open arms, and hearts of love?
They the blessèd ones gone before,
They the blessèd for evermore;
Out of great tribulation they went
Home to their home of heaven content.

What are these that fly as a cloud,
With flashing heads and faces bowed;
In their mouths a victorious psalm,
In their hands a robe and a palm?
Welcoming Angels these that shine,
Your own Angel, and yours and mine;
Who have hedged us, both day and night
On the left hand and on the right.

Light above light, and bliss beyond bliss,
Whom words cannot utter, lo, who is this?
As a King with many crowns he stands,
And our names are grav'n upon his hands;
As a Priest, with God-up-lifted eyes,
He offers for us his Sacrifice;
As the Lamb of God, for sinners slain,
That we too may live, he lives again.

God the Father give us grace
To walk in the light of Jesu's face;
God the Son give us a part
In the hiding-place of Jesu's heart;
God the spirit so hold us up
That we may drink of Jesu's cup;
God Almighty, God Three in One,
God Almighty, God alone.

CHRISTINA ROSSETTI (1830–1894)

Crucifixion. *Edward Burne-Jones*

Onward, Christian soldiers

Onward, Christian soldiers,
  Marching as to war,
With the Cross of Jesus
  Going on before.
Christ the royal Master
  Leads against the foe;
Forward into battle,
  See, his banners go!

> *Onward, Christian soldiers,*
>   *Marching as to war,*
> *With the Cross of Jesus*
>   *Going on before.*

At the sign of triumph
  Satan's legions flee;
On then, Christian soldiers,
  On to victory.
Hell's foundations quiver
  At the shout of praise;
Brothers, lift your voices,
  Loud your anthems raise.

Like a mighty army
  Moves the Church of God;
Brothers, we are treading
  Where the Saints have trod;
We are not divided,
  All one body we,
One in hope and doctrine
  One in charity.

Crowns and thrones may perish,
   Kingdoms rise and wane,
But the Church of Jesus
   Constant will remain;
Gates of hell can never
   'Gainst that Church prevail;
We have Christ's own promise,
   And that cannot fail.

Onward, then, ye people,
   Join our happy throng,
Blend with ours your voices
   In the triumph song;
Glory, laud, and honour
   Unto Christ the King;
This through countless ages
   Men and Angels sing.

SABINE BARING-GOULD (1834–1924)

Now the day is over

Now the day is over,
   Night is drawing nigh,
Shadows of the evening
   Steal across the sky.

Now the darkness gathers,
   Stars begin to peep,
Birds and beasts and flowers
   Soon will be asleep.

Jesu, give the weary
   Calm and sweet repose;
With thy tenderest blessing
   May our eyelids close.

Grant to little children
   Visions bright of thee;
Guard the sailors tossing
   On the deep blue sea.

Comfort every sufferer
   Watching late in pain;
Those who plan some evil
   From their sin restrain.

Christ in the house of His parents. *J E Millais*

Through the long night watches
    May thine Angels spread
Their white wings above me,
    Watching round my bed.

When the morning wakens,
    Then may I arise
Pure, and fresh, and sinless
    In thy holy eyes.

Glory to the Father,
    Glory to the Son,
And to thee, blest Spirit,
    Whilst all ages run.

SABINE BARING-GOULD (1834–1924)

Recessional

God of our fathers, known of old,
   Lord of our far-flung battle-line,
Beneath whose awful hand we hold
   Dominion over palm and pine –
Lord God of Hosts, be with us yet,
Lest we forget – lest we forget!

The tumult and the shouting dies;
   The captains and the kings depart:
Still stands thine ancient sacrifice,
   An humble and a contrite heart.
Lord God of Hosts, be with us yet,
Lest we forget – lest we forget!

Far-called, our navies melt away;
   On dune and headland sinks the fire:
Lo, all our pomp of yesterday
   Is one with Nineveh and Tyre!
Judge of the Nations, spare us yet,
Lest we forget – lest we forget!

If, drunk with sight of power, we loose
   Wild tongues that have not thee in awe.
Such boastings as the Gentiles use
   Or lesser breeds without the Law –
Lord God of Hosts, be with us yet
Lest we forget – lest we forget!

For heathen heart that puts her trust
   In reeking tube and iron shard,
All valiant dust that builds on dust,
   And guarding, calls not thee to guard,
For frantic boast and foolish word –
Thy mercy on thy people, Lord!

RUDYARD KIPLING (1865–1936)

The Dead Sea. *From an engraving after J M W Turner by W Finden*

The Authors

Ecce Ancilla Domini. *D G Rossetti*

The Artists